# CONTAINER GARDENING

**HOW TO QUICKLY GROW VEGETABLES, HERBS AND FRUITS A FEW STEPS FROM YOUR KITCHEN! TIPS ON HOW TO MANAGE PESTS OR OTHER DISEASES.**

## MEL EDWARDS

# TABLE OF CONTENTS

# INTRODUCTION

Container gardening can act as a starting point for those who're unsuccessful with keeping plants or haven't ever tried gardening. Pot gardening is such an easy process that even someone completely new to gardening can enjoy it. To get started, all you need is a pot, potting soil, and plants or plant seeds.

## Container Gardening is economical

The best part about container gardening is that you can pick up anything in which to grow your plant.

You only need to glance around your home and you're sure to find countless things that you can use as a container in which to build a beautiful garden. Simply grab the items, make holes for drainage in the bottom, fill them with compost and soil, add nasturtiums or pansies, and you're done. By just spending a small amount of money, you've made an attractive garden within your house.

## Space never matters

Even the tiniest place can be enhanced with a container garden. People grow lovely vegetable and flower gardens on stoops and fire escapes, for example. Despite space limitations, you can still build a container garden that will fit perfectly in any amount of space that you might have.

If your house is in a location where you don't get much sunlight, it is a good idea to get a terra cotta container filled with various colored coleus.

If the container is in direct contact with too much sunlight, fill the pot with succulents to build a beautiful garden that will more or less take care of itself.

## Grow a cactus garden anywhere

Container gardening is not restricted by geographical boundaries. You can grow a cactus in Alaska or a fern in the desert. All you need to do is to ensure that you have the correct plant for the particular spot that you have chosen, as there are a variety of conditions, such as warm, shady, sunny, cool, etc. If you don't have the right conditions outdoors, you can recreate them indoors.

## Children love this type of garden

Container gardens attract kids. Carrots can be much more appealing when kids can watch them growing on the balcony and can consume them when they are small and tasty. Kids love the content feeling that a container garden can provide them with, and they can take pride in growing a plant that their whole family can eat.

## Garden in a container to outsmart critters

People who grow tomatoes in the ground will be familiar with the problems that are faced when their plants are eaten by creatures. These people may then decide to move their plants to pots on their decks, where they cannot be reached, and then enjoy being able to consume every tomato from their plant.

## Container gardening can bring immediate happiness

Only a handful of things in life can provide you with the same level of gratification that a container garden gives. You can visit a nearby nursery, spend some time there, and pick out many healthy, flowering plants. Then, you simply have to fill the container with these plants, and you'll be gifted with a mind-blowing, skillful looking garden.

You can have containers able to survive winter, and at the same time bring lovely green accents to areas that would otherwise be boring and bland.

## Grow anything in a container garden

Let's just say that there's hardly any plant that cannot thrive in a pot garden. It is convenient to grow herbs, vegetables, and even trees in a garden designed inside a container.

## Container gardening can suit any personality

Container gardening allows you to aim for any style and intricacy of pot that you would like to. Two or three pansies inside a container may be more than enough to start with, or maybe you would like to do landscaping of the whole location with pots. To be a successful container gardener, all you need is patience, eagerness to experiment, and a love of having fun in the dirt.

# CHAPTER 1: WHY GROW PLANTS IN CONTAINERS?

Experienced gardeners say that container gardening can be tough, so you have to make the right choice of plants. A bit of research, training, and practical lessons from your friends and neighbors can be helpful. And reading seriously through this book will be informative and useful.

Container gardening can be profitable. You can sell one or two pots of grown and mature plants to your neighbors, and explore the business by selling through the Internet. This kind of business can expand depending on your creativity to generate beautiful container gardens for ornamental purposes. The right contacts can also lead to a successful venture. You can always target for at least 50% profit in a container gardening business.

You can sell container gardens of various types at prices ranging from $5 up. But you have to invest in a space where you can showcase your plants. Costs on seedlings and materials could be minimal. The marketing aspect is another story.

If you are successful in this venture, you can extend your business by publishing brochures and guidebooks that can be marketed as knowledge products; you can even produce film clips that can be a sure hit on the Internet.

Container gardening makes one's home attractive. Houses decorated by container gardens have no dull corners and bare walls because various ornamentals like ferns, palms, small flowering plants, and even herbs can be found mixed-and-matched with

the furniture and small pieces of home decors. There are also special container gardens reserved for specials occasions and family gatherings. These beautiful plants enliven and add to the party atmosphere during these special moments.

Indoor greeneries have a relaxing effect especially if these are well placed. This is true not only for the homes but also for offices and public places. Scientifically speaking, the oxygen that comes from the plant may be minimal to have a positive effect on body metabolism, but it is the sight of life that gives the relaxing effect. (There are species of plants like the snake plant that has been tested and proven to release a good amount of oxygen.) Symbolically, a plant that is growing healthy gives hope, and breaks the monotony of life at home, in the office, or any other public places.

Certain types of herbs are grown in container gardens because of their medicinal value. Lemongrass, aloe, Mexican sage, and artichoke are examples of medicinal herbs that are usually grown in containers. The benefits of medicinal herbs against commercial medicine are not just a matter of preference, but certain individuals have developed some allergies on manufactured medicines and hence advised to take natural medications instead.

Container gardening is the least expensive way to "go organics." You can have a vegetable salad container garden to ensure a supply of vegetables that are 100% free of chemicals. Hence for health buffs, to raise a container garden can provide savings since certified organic vegetables have higher prices compared to ordinary vegetables in supermarkets.

Container gardening can feed the world. It has been promoted by development advocates as one way to supplement the food of the poor. But the poorest among them cannot raise a single pot due to lack of space and sunshine in their homes. Nevertheless, for urban dwellers who have a bit of space, vegetable container gardening can be an option. They can raise beans, potato, pepper, and onion in window boxes or tin cans to be placed right at their doorstep.

Have you seen retirees and other elderly people spending so much time taking care of their container gardens? For them, pampering their container gardens is a productive and healthful past time. They can exercise and relax, and yes, socialize by having small gatherings to talk about their plants. The sight of window boxes with colorful petunias in their homes is a sight to behold, and their source of pride and joy. The activity provides sunshine and therapy to arthritic hands and the opportunity to stretch their backs.

# CHAPTER 2: GARDEN DESIGN

There are some things you'll need to get you going to get started in container gardening. The size of the containers you use will be determined by the kind of plants you would like to grow. The type of container you will choose will affect your garden design. Although there are many choices when it comes to containers and soil, my best piece of advice is to come up with a plan that you have for your container garden this year.

I also find that using your local gardening stores and online secondhand outlets list and Facebook marketplaces are good ways to find cost-effective containers and gardening supplies. If you want your plants to grow healthy and to provide an abundance of fruit, then you need to ensure the container in which you plant them is big enough. The bigger, the better. Large plants need a lot of space, and most roots need room to grow.

Avoid small containers, as they often can't absorb sufficient water to get through hot summer days. Plus, the bigger your container, the more plants you can cultivate! Use containers, baskets, boxes, bathtubs, and other tubs, and troughs, anything that holds the soil. Just be sure that there are drainage holes in the bottom.

Caring recommendations for container gardening with vegetables in ceramic pots are: they are generally more attractive than plastic pots, but plastic pots hold good moisture and will not dry out as rapidly as unglazed terracotta pots. Slip a plastic pot into a slightly larger clay one to get the best of both pots.

Black containers absorb heat when they're sitting in the sunlight. Most plants that grow in pots need to be watered as often as twice a day. Establish a container garden like in any other agribusiness company. The establishment of a container garden will begin with proper planning. Here are some different types of containers you will use to make smart decisions about what to plant in it.

# Where to place your containers?

You have two choices. The first is to place them wherever you want in the yard, making sure it is aesthetically pleasing. The other choice, the one we're going to talk about, is to carefully plan where to place your containers so that you can grow exactly what you want with the highest probability of success.

When you plan what you want to grow before you place the container in your yard, you can make sure you place it in the perfect space to provide the most amount of sun, shade, and wind protection that that species requires to thrive. So, carefully planning your space is what separates the beginners from the experts, and the best way to start your first garden is to do it like a true professional.

If you already have a clear idea of what you want to grow, then you should do some research and note down what temperature and amount of light you need. There will be a few factors that determine whether a place is right to place a container or not; how much sun and how much shade, the temperature of the place, protection from wind, protection from critters. So far, we have not considered the aesthetics of the place. However, this does not mean that this factor should not be considered, but rather that it is a consideration based on personal taste. I recommend that you evaluate all of these open and make a note of them on a piece of paper, so that you can use it as a guide when choosing where to place your containers.

At the top of the list you need to include how much sun or shade the place you have considered receives. Some plants, tomatoes for example, love to get lots of sun. That's how they turn a beautiful flaming red and that's a sign that they're ready to be harvested. However, there are exceptions. In fact, there are many other plants that don't need as much sun and prefer to grow in the shade. Lettuce is one such example. Lettuce likes to get some sun, but too much could ruin it.

To figure out how much sun or shade a location is getting, look at it over the course of the day. My advice is to check once every hour or two and realize how much sun it gets during the day. Pay particular attention in the afternoon. This is because the shade can come and go depending on what is casting it. Doing this will allow you to figure out exactly how much sun a certain location receives. Whether a place is shaded or not does not make it better or worse. It just changes the type of plants that can grow in that location.

While you're checking the sun during the day, I recommend checking the temperature as well. Stick the thermometer in the ground and see how warm the soil is when the sun is beating down. Do the same when there is shade. Take one last reading just before you go to sleep. This will allow you to gather some very important data. You can note the difference between a space in shade and one in full sun to get an idea of the various temperatures your plants will face.

## Choosing Containers

The layout of the containers to be chosen and used is a demonstration of the design objectives set by the gardener based on his/her bias and the availability of these materials. If, for example, it is intended to display containers, glazed ceramic pots, porcelain pots, and plastic pots in all sizes and shapes may be used. With some talent, the native materials available in the locality can be transformed into gorgeously looking containers, like cut wooden poles or others. Only the imagination of the grower sets the boundaries. If the aim is to recycle and make long term use of objects that are usually dumped into the trash, then use old tires, sacks, soda cans, plastic bottles, etc.

The most readily available containers involve medium-sized plastic, much used only to hold ice cream or any other food products, and five-gallon transparent plastic containers that can be acquired from restaurants, bakeries, or marketplaces (wash containers with soap and warm water before use). The total depth and width of the container will be determined by what you plan to plant.

## Container Types Based on Material

Every element needs to be considered when choosing containers for your container garden. There is an almost endless number of professionally manufactured garden containers on the marketplace and an equivalent number of reprocessed products that could be turned into increasing containers. Growing product has its pro's and con's, and so each consideration must be acknowledged when determining which sorts of containers are worth investing in.

It is possible to use containers made of clay, wood, plastic, or metal for growing vegetables. Consider also the use of barrels, flower pots, or hanging baskets. Unusual containers are going to add interest to your garden. Here are some of the most common

garden container materials and a list of reasons to remember when making your decisions.

## 1. <u>Terra-cotta Containers</u>:

Photo by <u>Maggie Hoffman</u> on <u>Foter.com</u> / <u>CC BY</u>

They look gorgeous in the garden, but they also have their major disadvantage as clay pots can also develop white salt blemishes on the outside and change color moss. Clay absorbs heat, too, a significant benefit in the spring, but not as effective in the summer when the atmosphere in the container can get too dry.

They could be costlier and heavier to shift and more fragile. They also appear to be very hot.

## 2. Ceramic Glazed Containers:

Photo by john bonham2 on Foter.com / CC BY-SA

They also look attractive and beautiful again in the garden, but they are also breakable. Ceramic glazed garden containers are available in many sizes, styles, designs, and colors. These are also made with the same fine-textured clay that has been fired in a kiln and glazed with wires. They typically hold moisture a little better because of the glaze on the container, and, usually, won't get as hot as the terra-cotta containers. But they're generally more expensive.

## 3. Plastic:

During the last few decades, gardening through plastic containers and pots has come a significant way. By using the trendy shades and patterns, it allows the containers to appear more attractive. Plastic is supposed to be the easiest option, and the lightest one to shift around. In comparison with terra-cotta or ceramic pots, these plastic containers are very sturdy and much less likely to break. My only concern with plastic containers is they are considered as reusable, so when you choose to buy them for your garden, ensure you utilize them year by year. Good insulation properties are seen in this type of container, as well as strong soil moisture retention. It's necessary to paint a high-quality exterior to restore their appearance.

## 4. <u>Wood</u>:

Especially in the case of planning your wood garden, wood planter boxes are very affordable and easily accessible. Wooden containers, particularly raised bed containers, gives a lovely look in the garden. The casual, natural presentation of wood relates itself perfectly to both cottage-style gardens and residential landscapes.

## 5. Cement Containers:

Photo by thegardenbuzz on Foter.com / CC BY-ND

Cement planters are costly, but they are extremely durable. They're heavy, however, particularly once the soil has been added to them, so you're better off choosing more permanent containers that you don't intend to move around.

At the end of the day, almost anything can be turned into a container, and I love the unexpected options for bringing some character to your garden. The most important key

point is that whatever you use, it is huge enough for your plants.

| Lettuce | Cilantro |
|---------|----------|
| Spinach | Sage |
| Mint | Cherry tomatoes |
| Basil | Strawberries |
| Nasturtiums | Bush/Hanging cucumbers |

Herbs and plants growing in window boxes

# 6. <u>Window Box Container</u>:

Photo by <u>sharon_k</u> on <u>Foter.com</u> / <u>CC BY-SA</u>

A large window box can create a handy salad within reach of your arm! Whatever the size or type, place your containers where they are most convenient to be cared for and grow best. Many vegetables need 6 to 8 hours of direct sunlight to thrive and produce well. Plants in containers need the best soil, aeration, and drainage for healthy root growth and ideal harvesting.

# Patio Container:

Photo by jeffreyw on Foter.com / CC BY

Below are a few of my favorite plants that we grow in our patio container garden and that do really well!

| | |
|---|---|
| Poll beans | Sage |
| Spinach | Cilantro |
| Lettuce | Tarragon |
| Swiss chard | Thyme |
| Cherry tomatoes | Lavender |
| Vine tomatoes | Rosemary |
| Eggplant | Basil |

## Container Size

Containers will entirely depend on the plant you're currently growing. Sometimes the required container size will be shown on your seed packet, but I want to give you a good idea of the general container sizes needed for different herbs and vegetables.

Choose a container that is big enough to hold the plants and satisfy their root systems. Plastic or clay pots, aged pails, gallons, plastic containers, washtubs, wooden planters, or window boxes are used to hold vegetable plants. Almost every form of container may be used if it provides excellent drainage through holes on the sides or below.

If holes are needed, drill four or even more 1/4-inch holes uniformly spaced across the bottom of the container. For more drainage, place about 1/2 inch of rough sand, small rocks, or pieces of broken clay pot at the bottom of each container (but these components are not a replacement for drainage holes).

The diameter and number of containers you need depend on the space available and the vegetables you plan to grow. Six to ten-inch diameter pots are suitable for chips, parsley, herbs, or miniature tomato plants such as 'Pixie Hybrid.' For most vegetable crops such as tomatoes, peppers, and eggplant, a 3 to 5-gallon container is preferred. (See Table 1). Lumber containers will last longer if they are manufactured of the heartwood of naturally sustainable tree species, like western red cedar and redwood.

Treated timber is a different option. Timber that is treated with chromed copper arsenate is suggested for structures that come into contact with soil. The CCA timber chemical is forced into the wood under a pressure treatment process where it is fixed to the wood and remains permanently. CCA cannot leach from a well dried treated wood and is rarely harmful to plants. The existence of CCA treated wood in contact with soil is 40 years. It has a slightly green shade and is sold to be used as landscape wood, fences, and decks.

The container should be of the correct size for the plant growing in it (see Table 1 for the types and sizes of growing containers).

| Vegetables | Container sizes | No. Of plants |
|---|---|---|
| Lettuce | 10 inches | 2 plants |
| Broccoli | 2 gallons | 1 plant |
| Carrot | 1 gallon | 2-3 plants |
| Onions | 1 gallon | 3-5 plants |
| Green Bean | 2 gallons | Space plants 3 inches apart |
| Cucumber | 1 gallon | 1 plant |
| Beets | 2 gallons | Thinned to 2-3 inches apart |
| Cabbage | 1 gallon | 1 plant |
| Carrots | 2 gallons | Thinned to 2-3 inches apart |
| Cucumber | 2 gallons | 2 plants |
| Eggplant | 1 gallon | 1 plant |
| Green beans | 1 gallon | 2-3 plants |
| Leaf lettuce | 1/2 gallon | 4-6 plants |
| Parsley | 2 gallons | 3 plants |
| Pepper | 2 gallons | 2 plants |
| Radishes | 1 gallon | Thinned to 1-2 inches apart |
| Spinach | 1 gallon | Thinned to 3 inches apart |
| Swiss chard | 1 gallon | 1 plant |
| Tomatoes | 3 gallons | 1 plant |
| Cherry | 2 gallons | 1 plant |
| Turnip | 2 gallons | 2 plants |

**Table 1. Approximate size containers needed for vegetables**

# CHAPTER 3: SELECTION OF PLANTS

## Vegetables to grow

There are many vegetables that you can grow in a container; Basically, you can grow almost anything you want. Here's a list of what crops are best suited for container gardening.

## Root vegetables

Root vegetables like carrots and beets and radishes do well in containers. Carrots develop deep roots, so you need a fairly deep container, say about 8 to 12 inches. Vegetables with deeper roots will not grow if you have a shallow container. So favor deeper containers (12" is fine) to grow deep-rooted vegetables.

Since containers tend to be rock-free, you'll have good quality carrots with long, well-formed roots. Add horticultural sand to the containers to make them drain better, so the carrots will grow straighter.

Potatoes, however, are not particularly suited to containers. In fact, the potatoes will grow into the soil underneath and you'll need a lot of digging to get them out. In larger containers, you'll have to practically empty the pot to get all the potatoes out. This is a personal preference; there are some people who plant potatoes in containers, but I prefer to grow them in bags. The advantage of growing in bags is that you don't find potato plants showing up in containers the next year, and you don't have to do much digging to get them out of the ground.

However, if you want to grow potatoes in a container, then you need the soil to be 18-24 inches deep. That doesn't necessarily mean it won't work! You may have a good crop of potatoes but my personal preference is to avoid it because of the digging required...it's much easier to empty a bag! Also, for years afterwards, you will find potatoes growing in the container that will disturb your other vegetable crops.

## Leafy vegetables

Most leafy greens such as kale, spinach, cauliflower, lettuce and so on can be planted in a container and will grow just fine. Many of these can be started early in the year, while some, such as kale, cauliflower, broccoli and others can be started later in the year and overwintered. Because containers heat up faster than the surrounding soil, you can often get a good crop before summer. Also, containers are especially good because they promote drainage.

You should be aware that they will suffer attacks from pests, particularly slugs and caterpillars. A tight mesh cage built over the container will keep these types of animals away. Also, young plants are at risk of damage from birds, so they also need a cover; you could use a plastic polytunnel.

## Onions, Leeks and Garlic

All members of the onion family do well in a container, because they like plenty of organic matter and draining soil. Regarding their growing season you should know that, grown from seed, they can take more than 100 days to mature.

The onion family does not like competition and this can cause their death. Be sure to keep the weeds down because they will surround the onions. In hot weather, I recommend watering these plants daily to prevent them from over-drying and consequently dying.

## Tomatoes

Tomatoes are greedy for food and, I recommend adding extra compost to your container so they will grow even faster. However, the real problem is planting the tomatoes because the support stakes are not firm enough in the loose soil. I recommend securing the stakes to the edges of the container. Tomatoes ripen with heat and not just the sun, so you may need to cover your tomato container to give them some extra warmth, particularly towards the end of the growing season. You can use clear plastic to keep them warm so they produce a good crop.

## Peas and beans

These will grow very well in raised beds. However, you may have trouble supporting taller crops. I recommend attaching supports to the container, this will help!

Young plants are at risk of bird attacks, so it's good to have them covered and protected. With beans you'll need to build a frame out of bamboo canes, using 10 to 12 foot tall canes.

Peas also need support. You can make a net out of garden twine to do this, so the pea plants will use it for support. Putting a six-foot bamboo cane in each corner plus one in the middle will allow you to build a net of twine that will support your peas. Add more canes as needed.

## Vine crops

These are not very suitable for raised beds, particularly since pumpkins are really very greedy for food. The problem with this type of plant is that they can crowd out neighboring plants. You could build supports and grow the cucumbers vertically, which helps reduce the space needed.

## Growing Herbs

Herbs do not need to be part of a crop rotation scheme. Many herbs are annuals and will need to be reseeded each year, but others are perennials and can remain in place permanently with some pruning at the end of each growing season.

Laurel, lavender, marjoram, rosemary, thyme and many others will last for many years. Remember that laurels are just that...trees, and so they grow very tall unless they are pruned and kept in check. Rosemary and lavender both benefit from a good pruning at the end of the growing season, otherwise they become woody and with fewer flowers.

Herbs that have similar soil requirements should be grown together. Plants that like dry soil will not thrive in the same pot as plants that prefer a wetter growing environment. So, I recommend grouping plants that have similar needs together.

Unless you live in an area with lots of sun, basil will be happiest under glass. It is a biennial plant, although it is treated as an annual in colder areas. However, it loves the sun and will do very well in your greenhouse along with your tomatoes.

Mint, lemon balm and other members of the mint family should not be planted in the ground because they are incredibly invasive and will crowd out other herbs and plants. These herbs are best grown in pots to keep them contained and prevent them from spreading.

**Growing flowers in containers**

Containers are ideal for growing flowers.

As with most other plants, different flowers prefer different soil types and conditions. By grouping flowers with similar needs in the same container, you will ensure beautiful blooms.

It is important to remember that your flowers will grow the container. At first, you need to leave enough space between each plant so that it can grow without crowding out other flowers. As with herbs, your pots will look bare at first, but avoid the temptation to fill the space, the plants will expand and your pot will burst with color.

# Broad Beans-Lima

Light Requirements: Full sun

Spacing: Sow seeds 3" apart, 1" deep

Container: 2-gal container minimum size

Varieties: Ford hook 242 (AAS) - The standard for Lima beans for more than 60 years

Comments: Limas like more heat than regular bush beans and will bear poorly in cool weather.

# Broad Beans-Fava

Photo by Dinesh Valke on Foter.com / CC BY-SA

<u>Light Requirements:</u> Full sun

<u>Spacing:</u> Sow seeds 3" apart, 1" deep

<u>Container:</u> 2-gal container minimum size

<u>Varieties:</u> Windsor-A classic English variety

<u>Comments:</u> Prefers cool mild conditions and are suitable for early spring and fall planting. Aphids love fava beans, so watch diligently for this insect and get rid of them immediately.

# Broccoli

<u>Light Requirements</u>: Full sun

<u>Spacing</u>: 1 plant per pot

<u>Container</u>: 2-gal container minimum size for 1 plant

<u>Varieties</u>: Bonanza, Packman

<u>Comments</u>: Pot should be 12-14" deep. Watch for white butterflies around flowering heads. These will lay eggs and turn into cabbage worms. They can be picked off as you see them. Heads can be protected with cheesecloth if you wish.

# Beans

<u>Light Requirements</u>: Full sun

<u>Spacing</u>: Sow seeds 3" apart, 1" deep

<u>Container</u>: 2-gal container minimum size

<u>Varieties</u>: Bean Beananza, Jade, Blue Lake

<u>Comments</u>: Bean Beananza is a dwarf French bean that produces twice as long as most beans. It is available from Burpee seed. Harvest regularly to encourage pod setting.

# Filet Beans (Haricot Verts)

Photo by sharon_k on Foter.com / CC BY-SA

Light Requirements: Full sun

Spacing: Sow seeds 3" apart, 1" deep

Container: 2-gal container minimum size

Varieties: Maxibel, Tavera French Filet Stringless

Comments: Filet beans are intended to be picked when they are very slim 1/8"-1/4" in diameter. Their gourmet appearance makes them very appealing to gourmet chefs. Pick every 3 days to maintain the continuous production of slim beans. Not recommended for freezing or canning

# Carrots

<u>Light Requirements</u>: Full sun/Tolerates partial shade

<u>Spacing</u>: 1 1/2 -3" in a row. Thin early to avoid tangled roots.

<u>Container</u>: 24 X 36 X 10" box or minimum 1-gallon single container

<u>Varieties</u>: Little Finger (H), Baby Spike, Thumbelina, Nantes Half Long (H), Royal Chantenay, Caracas (H)

<u>Comments</u>: Carrots are slow-growing so weeding is very important for optimum crop performance. Loose soil is required. Choose short-rooted varieties for container gardening such as Nantes Half Long or Royal Chantenay. The image shown is Caracas available from Burpee Seed. This is a new hybrid gourmet baby carrot that is ideal for container growing. Use pots 2-3" deeper than carrot depth.

# Cucumbers

Light Requirements: Full sun

Spacing: 12-16" apart 1 plant per gallon

Container: 48" box or a 5-gal container with a trellis

Varieties: Diva (AAS), Rocky (baby cukes) Picklebush, Baby Cucumber Patio Pik, and Salty are bush types and produce on vines only 18-24" long

Comments: Requires hot weather. Provide support for climbing vines. The image shown is Baby Cucumber, a gourmet cucumber available from Park Seed.

# Eggplant

Light Requirements: Full Sun

Spacing: One plant per container

Container: 4-5 gallons containers

Varieties: Mission Bell (early), Black Beauty (H), Fairy Tale (AAS), Shooting Stars

Comments: In containers, the varieties with small fruit carried high on the plant are more interesting. Eggplants are very ornamental and look well when planted alongside flowers in larger planters. The image shown is Shooting Stars, an eggplant bred for container gardening available from Burpee Seed.

34

# Garlic

<u>Light Requirements</u>: Full sun

<u>Spacing</u>: 4-6" apart 1 1/2-2" deep

<u>Container</u>: 1/2 gallons container 8" deep

<u>Varieties</u>: Italian Loiacono (H),

<u>Comments</u>: Garlic is planted in the fall. It is very winter hardy but should be mulched to prevent heaving. Harvest in the summer when the bottom 2-3 leaves have yellowed.

# Green Onions (Scallions)

<u>Light Requirements</u>: Full Sun/Partial shade

<u>Spacing</u>: 2" apart in a 48" box -- 3-5 plants per 1-gallon container

<u>Container</u>: Any container 6-8" deep

<u>Varieties</u>: Evergreen Bunching, Crystal Wax, Guardsman (earliest bunching onion) Italian Red of Florence (H).

<u>Comments</u>: Scallions are immature onions. Seed can be sown in early spring for summer use or in July or August for fall use. For the earliest harvest, sow seeds inside about a month before the last frost. Sow several plantings a few weeks apart to get a constant harvest throughout the summer.

Bunching onions never develop a bulb and are commonly known as scallions. Mount up more soil along the base as the scallion grows to get a large section of white onion.

## Green Peas

Photo by Biscarotte on Foter.com / CC BY-SA

Light Requirements: Full sun

Spacing: 2"-3" apart

Container: 2"-3" apart in a 48" box — or any container 8" deep

Varieties: Sugar Snap, Little Marvel, Tom Thumb, Early Frosty, Oregon Sugar Pod (Snow Pea)

Comments: If you've only eaten canned or frozen peas in your lifetime, you are missing out on one of the world's most flavorful vegetables. There is nothing to compare with the sweet taste of early peas. When we had our garden, we couldn't keep the kids from eating fresh peas right from the pod. It was really hard to get enough for a meal. You'll never know the taste of fresh peas unless you grow them because the sugar turns to starch as soon as they are picked. If you haven't eaten them freshly picked from the vine, you'll never experience the true taste of a fresh pea.

Peas can be directly sown into the container and harvested by early summer. Plant peas in containers when the temperature reaches 45 degrees. Set along a wall or trellis.

38

# Kale

Photo by www.metaphoricalplatypus.com on Foter.com /
CC BY

Light Requirements: Full sun/Partial shade

Spacing: 8"-12" apart

Container: 12 x 48" box or 5 gallons container

Varieties: Dwarf Blue Curled Vates, Red Russin (H)

Comments: Grows best in cool days of fall. Harvest leaves as soon as they are large

enough. Cut the whole plant if desired.

# Lettuce

<u>Light Requirements:</u> Full sun/Partial shade

<u>Spacing</u>: Leaf lettuce-4-6" Head lettuce-10"

<u>Container</u>: Head lettuce needs room - 48" box Leaf lettuce-any container will do

<u>Varieties</u>: Summer Bibb, Buttercrunch, Oakleaf, Slobolt

<u>Comments</u>: Sow leaf lettuce at 2-week intervals to keep harvesting. Seeds germinate best if sown along with ice cubes. High temperatures cause lettuce to bolt (flower). Varieties listed above are slow to bolt.

With healthy eating being in the spotlight today, the varieties of lettuce are being expanded in seed catalogs at a rapid pace. Check garden centers and seed catalogs for new mixes and varieties that are being introduced every spring. Image sown is Buttercrunch.

# Peppers-Hot

Photo by LivewithoutPS on Foter.com / CC BY-ND

Light Requirements: Full sun

Spacing: 14-18" apart in a row -- 1 plant per 2-4 gallons container

Container: 48" box -- 2-4 gallons container

Varieties: Ancho (H), Hungarian Hot Wax, Krimzon Lee, Hot Lemon (H)

Comments: Not only for cooking, but these peppers are also a great ornamental vegetable. They will fit in well when planted with flowers. Available in all shapes and colors and degrees of heat.

# Peppers-Sweet

<u>Light Requirements</u>: Full sun

<u>Spacing</u>: 14-18" apart in a row -- 1 plant per 4-5 gallons container

<u>Container</u>: 48" box -- 2-4 gallons container

<u>Varieties</u>: Ace (Green-exceptionally early, cold tolerant), Gourmet (Yellow), Tangerine Dream (red-orange 18" bush), Sweet Banana (Yellow - H, Lipstick (Red)

<u>Comments</u>: Easy to grow but not much difference in flavor from store-bought produce. Peppers are a great ornamental vegetable that will fit in well when planted with flowers. Peppers come in all shapes and colors.

# Potatoes

<u>Light Requirements</u>: Full sun

<u>Spacing</u>: 1 seed potato per bucket

<u>Container</u>: 5-gallon bucket

<u>Varieties</u>: Yukon Gold, Red Pontiac, Kennebec, Green Mountain (H), Russet Burbank (H)

<u>Comments</u>: Many people love to grow a few potatoes in containers. Once again, the store-bought produce cannot compare to the flavor of homegrown potatoes. If you'd like to try growing potatoes in containers, there are many ways of doing this.

# Radishes

Light Requirements: Full Sun/Partial shade

Spacing: Sow seeds 3/4-1" apart - 1/2" deep

Container: Gallon containers 8" deep or long boxes 24-48"

Varieties: Cherry Belle, White Icicle, Watermelon (H)

Comments: Water often to keep radishes mild, tender, and attractive. Radishes remain in prime condition only a few days. Be diligent about harvesting to avoid pithy, tough, spicy radishes. Image shown – Easter Egg Blend from Park Seed Company Shallots

# Onions

<u>Light Requirements</u>: Full sun

<u>Spacing</u>: Space bulbs about 6" apart.

<u>Container</u>: 48" box -- 2-4 gallons container

<u>Varieties</u>: Ambition, Dutch Yellow, Holland Red

<u>Comments:</u> Shallots are a gourmet alternative to garlic and very pricey in the grocery store, so pricey you'll probably get sticker shock if you've never looked at them before now. If you've purchased them in a grocery store, you'll be surprised at the flavor of a freshly picked shallot as compared to what's available in the produce section.

Shallots are easy to grow from seed in containers and very productive. However, they are most often grown from bulbs. If you want to grow them from seed, Ambition is the variety to try. It is available from Park Seed.

# Spinach

<u>Light Requirements</u>: Full sun/Partial shade

<u>Spacing</u>: 8-10" apart in rows, 2 plants per gallon

<u>Container</u>: 48" box, gallon container

<u>Varieties</u>: Emu and Tyee (both very slow bolting) All varieties grow well in containers.

<u>Comments</u>: Spinach germinates best in cool weather. Plant spinach early in spring. In some areas, it may also be sown in September for an early crop in the spring. Check with your local nursery or extension office to see if this can be done in your area. Be sure to mulch heavily to protect the fall planting.

# Summer Squash – Zucchini

<u>Light Requirements</u>: Full sun

<u>Spacing</u>: 1 plant per container

<u>Container</u>: 5-gallon container

<u>Varieties</u>: Ford hook (Zucchini Bush Plant), Saffron (Summer Squash Bush Plant)

<u>Comments:</u> Look for bush-type varieties for your containers if you don't have room for your plants to roam or plant along walls with a wire trellis for support. Many people think summer squash and zucchini are different vegetables, but they are all the same family – summer squash.

# Swiss chard

<u>Light Requirements</u>: Full sun

<u>Spacing:</u> 4-5" apart thin to 12" apart

<u>Container</u>: Any container 6-8" deep

<u>Varieties</u>: Bright Lights (AAS), Neon Lights (Rainbow Colors Mix)

<u>Comments:</u> Only one planting is needed. Outer leaves may be harvested as soon as they are big enough and can be harvested until frost. Perfect "cut and come again" plant. The image shown is a variety of Bright Lights, available from Burpee. This is a beautiful eye-catching vegetable for containers.

# Tomatoes

<u>Light Requirements</u>: Full sun

<u>Spacing</u>: 1 plant per container

<u>Container</u>: 15 gallons

<u>Varieties</u>: Pixie, Patio, Tiny Tim, Saladette, Tumblin" Tom (Great for hanging baskets), Brandywine (H)

<u>Comments</u>: Tomatoes are the most popular vegetables grown in containers. There are hundreds of varieties available. Check your local garden centers and seed catalogs for up to date information on the latest offerings of new varieties. The image shown is Brandywine, one of the most flavorful heirloom tomatoes available.

# CHAPTER 4: SOIL PREPARATION

The soil is mainly composed of mineral, nutrients, residues of plants and animals, water and other inorganic particles. The best soil for vegetables and fruits is loamy soil, a mixture of clay, sand, silt and additional organic matter. What makes it a very fertile soil is the combination of all these elements that disengage the negative properties of each one of them. Clay soil or sandy soil is not appropriate for growing vegetables due to their low level of nutrient properties and their inability to retain water, which makes it hard for the roots of our plants to absorb the needed water. But combined they create a very befitting soil for our needs.

First of all, we must prepare our growing spot. An important aspect of preparing the soil is cleaning the space that we will use for growing our plants.

If you have only the balcony at your disposal, there's not much preparation to do, since you will use special containers and you will buy the needed soil and fertilizers in specialized stores. These are things that don't need additional work, because they already contain all useful nutrient properties and do not require weed treatment or any other intervention, except for our use of imagination in creating the ultimate relaxing and useful own corner of bliss.

In our backyard, we may find a bit more work to do before starting growing our vegetables and fruits. The first thing to do is to turn the soil. It is an indispensable action for maintaining and enriching the nutritional reserves of the soil. Traditional gardeners recommend deep digging, while ecologists certainly go for the superficial one.

Their main argument for supporting their theory is that the superficial digging does not alter the life of the microorganisms and bacteria that live underground and have an essential role in keeping a biodynamic balance of the soil and respects the natural resources of it.

Cleaning the soil means getting rid of any small or large stone that we find, since they have a bad influence on the growing process of the plants, especially for those with pivoting roots. Discarding any weed root that we find is also highly recommended, especially when it comes to couch grass, which is our number one enemy in terms of growing vegetables, fruits and flowers.

Loosening the soil is an important stage of our project, since it allows our plants to make the best of the nutrient properties of the piece of land required for our vertical garden. It's all about grinding our soil. Doing this, we make it easier for our plants to obtain the best nutrient properties and the needed amount of water from the soil, hence achieving better growing results.

If you live in an apartment, the first thing to do is buy the best soil with the highest amount of nutrient properties. The more varied properties it has, the largest variety of plants we can grow in it. You should only know what plant you are interested in growing so that your provider can help you choose what is best for your needs.

You can find special soil for each plant, or a universal one. In the store, you can find all sorts of soils intended for vegetables, for fruits, for flowers, and for any other plant that you may want to grow. You can find natural or industrial types of fertilizers and you can also make your own compost. More on that later!

If you have a small garden, then you must prepare the soil first. An important matter is the type of soil that you have and what you must do to optimize it. There are available tests for finding out the nutrient properties and the pH level of the soil. The alkaline soils, or the slightly acidic soils, are the best ones for agriculture. Once you find out what pH level your soil has, you know what you have to do to make it fit. For example, if the pH level of your soil is higher than 7, 0, you deal with calcareous soil and if it's lower than 6, 0, then you deal with acidic soil. In the first case, please take into account that you should never add calcium oxide to it.

A simple and easy method of finding out the pH level of your soil is conducting a little experiment on your own, like in the old days of elementary school during chemistry or physics class. First of all, you must take samples of the soil, digging at approximately 11 or 23 inches deep. Mix all the samples and add some drops of vinegar. If the soil is calcareous, effervescence is spotted.

Another important aspect of your soil is whether it is soft soil or heavy soil. Figuring this out requires only 5 minutes. Grab a fistful of your soil and moisten it with water. Start kneading it, and if it shatters, then you have soft soil, which rapidly absorbs water. If, in turn, your result is a hardball, then you have heavy soil.

Another easy way of finding out what type of soil you have is by looking at your field after a few rainy days. If you see puddles of water on top, your soil is a heavy one, because it doesn't allow water to easily find its way through.

When dealing with soft soils, you must loosen it. It is advisable to turn your soil in the spring, because during the winter the soil is protected by a rich layer of leaves and other organic matters or compost, while consolidating with natural fertilizers, like manure.

For the heavy soils, turning should be done in autumn, followed by spreading manure or compost on top.

To obtain a nutrient and rich soil, you must consider some additional elements that will make your soil happy. These supplements are not fertilizers, they are a simple method of creating the perfect soil with the needed balance of properties. They are:

**Calcium oxide**. This is used on clay soils to make them easier to labor. At the same time, it decreases the acidity of the soil, which makes it harder for weeds to settle. It is beneficial for any type of soil, except for the calcareous one, as I already mentioned above.

**Moss**. This is a leafy-stemmed, flowerless plant that we find in tufts, mats, or moist grounds. It doesn't have nutrient properties, but it is used for retaining water since it behaves like a sponge and is better used for the easy soils that cannot retain water.

**Manure**. This is the only soil supplement that may also be considered a fertilizer. There are two types of manure: cold and hot. The cold one comes from cows, chickens, or rabbits and the hot ones from sheep and horse manure. The hot manure is beneficial for clay soils and the cold for calcareous soils. The important thing is not to use fresh manure, because it burns the roots of plants. It must be put aside in the field for at least three months. You may use it as a supplement once every three years.

For small gardens or balconies, it's always better to use organic manure granules. In this way, we get rid of the "stinky" issue of using natural fertilizers.

Some shops will provide you with natural fertilizers that contain the right amount of nutrient elements that our plants need. Even if there is a big difference between the needs of each plant; all of them need nitrogen (N), phosphorus (P), and potassium (K). These are the most significant elements that our fertilizer should contain.

**Nitrogen (N)**

Nitrogen's main action concerns the aerial part of the plants, meaning the stems and leaves. That's why it is a good fertilizer for all vegetables with big leaves like salad, spinach, or cabbage. In the past few years, its use as a vegetable fertilizer has increased due to the growth of the world population and the increased amount of food needed worldwide.

Lack of nitrogen causes the slow growth of the plants; excess causes frailty, makes the flowering and fruiting stop, along with causing a deficiency in fighting pests and diseases.

## Phosphorus (P)

Its main action is involved in the development of roots, flowers, seeds, and fruits and in increasing the resistance of the plants against pests and diseases. It is recommended for growing tomatoes, peppers, eggplants, fruit trees and flowers.

Lack of phosphorus causes decreased flowering and longer ripening time.

## Potassium (K)

This element is useful for strong stem growth, promotion of flowering and fruiting and the movement of water in plants. It favors root growth; it gives a better taste to fruits and more color to the flowers. It is beneficial for the uptake of nutrients.

Lack of potassium causes necrosis of the leaves and deficiency in fighting pests and diseases.

These three elements are complementary, and they should be used after proper transformation done by microorganisms, therefore the importance of compost.

## Animal-based fertilizers:

- Chicken manure. It is high in nitrogen and phosphorus. It's for the best to spread it on top of your soil at the beginning of spring. One handful of it should be more than enough for 10 square feet. You may easily consolidate it with the soil by using a rake.

- Guano. This is bat or seabird manure, which comes in pellet form or powdered. They are also high in nitrogen. You may use it exactly like the chicken manure.

- Poultry dry blood. It is the powdered blood of slaughtered animals; it contains a high amount of nitrogen and it favors plant growth. You should spread 400 grams on a surface of 10 square feet.

- Grounded or burned animal horns. They are rich in nitrogen. 400 grams should be more than enough for 10 square feet.

- Fishbone. They are very rich in phosphorus and are a universal fertilizer. You should use them in autumn or winter, by burying them at approximately 11 inches depth. From this category, you may also choose: fish emulsion-a liquid product that mixed with water is very effective for stimulating the growth of seedlings and hydrolyzed fish powder-it is rich in nitrogen, you should mix it with water and then spray it on the plants

# CHAPTER 5: FEED THE GARDEN

Photo by Ivan Radic on Foter.com / CC BY

When fertilizing your container plants, it is helpful to know the requirements of your plants. Some plants require alkaline soil while others prefer acidic soil. The only way to know what each plant prefers is to research the plants you have decided to use. This information is often on the plant label or seed packet, but if it isn't listed, you can check the plant name on the Internet or in your gardening books. Be sure to select compatible plants in this area when potting up a garden container to promote the correct growing conditions.

If you are planting your containers with a commercial mix, the nutrients needed for plant growth and health are incorporated into the mix. This should be good for 3-4 weeks. Because watering leaches fertilizer, how often you water should determine how often you fertilize your container plants.

Fertilizer is leached out of soilless potting mixes more quickly than other potting soils. For this reason, additional fertilizer is important when using this type of mix. There are many types of timed-released fertilizers, such as sticks and pellets that are available for use in containers. Just insert these into the soil and forget them. Be sure to check the labels for fertilizer information.

Some container gardeners prefer to fertilize container gardens with a weak solution every other watering. If this is a method you prefer, use only 1/4 of the solution called for in a monthly application. Plants in containers need more nutrients than those planted in a garden because of the small volume of soil in the container and also the frequent watering schedule that is required. It is necessary to compensate for the smaller root area by a more frequent watering and feeding schedule.

No plant requires a large amount of fertilizer at one time, but by continuously feeding your plants on a regular schedule, you will encourage lush growth and a continuous display of color. Do remember that smaller pots and lighter soil will need to be fertilized more frequently than larger pots filled with heavy soil, as frequent watering leaches nutrients out of the soil.

It's a good policy to fertilize your plants in the morning. As the sunlight and heat increase, plants start what is called "transpiration", the process of releasing moisture through their leaves. As this moisture is evaporated, more moisture is absorbed by the roots, thereby carrying the fertilizer to all parts of the plant.

Never fertilize your container gardens when the soil is dry. Fertilizer that touches dry roots may shock your plants. Be sure the soil is moist before you fertilize your container plants; a plant with moist roots is at the optimum level for taking in nutrients.

If you've been having a lot of rain, you may feel your plants are just fine and begin to neglect them. Your plants still need fertilizer even though the soil is moist. A plant can starve to death in a moist potting soil if you don't add fertilizer. Remember, the plants are growing in a crowded, limited space and each of them is fighting for nutrients to stay viable. Do not stop your fertilizing schedule just because you are having a rainy spell.

# CHAPTER 6: HOW TO TAKE CARE OF YOUR GARDEN

Creating a container garden is a big process. It starts with planning the types of plants to grow, the containers, the place to position them and decorating them, without disturbing the décor of the house. After going through all these steps, it is important to take good care of the container garden to gain the beauty of the plants. Caring would include watering, fertilizing, cleaning and preparing the plant to thrive in different climates.

## Change in climate

You cannot expect the climate to be constant. Moreover, you also ought to know that small containers won't be as resistant to climate change as large containers. The dried plant debris might change the color of the water and cause sediments in the containers. Wash, rinse and refill the containers. During the onset of winter, the water containers that are capable of resisting freezing should be insulated. You can better place the water container at the bottom of your swimming pool so that the water around the container would not freeze. During a warm climate, you should not add fertilizers to the plants. If you are growing tropical fish in your water container, ensure that you have a heat insulation system in place.

## Care when you are gone for long

During vacations or times when you are not available to water your garden, the chances of the container garden perishing are very high. This is one of the main reasons why most people do not want to start a garden. Drip irrigation is the best way to take care of your plants when you are away for a week.

Buy small plastic containers or use plastic containers. Place one plastic bottle in each container. Fill the plastic bottle with water and prick at the bottom, with a sharp needle. The water in the bottle would drain drop by drop into the containers.

If you are going away for a couple of days, the crystals can be used to give adequate water to your plants. You can buy these crystals from nurseries. The crystals would absorb the water and help the plant to retain humidity.

Photo by Michael Lehet on Foter.com / CC BY-ND

The other strategies including placing the containers in the shade or using a fountain to water all your plants, at the required interval! The best way is to ask your neighbor's kid to water your plants, in exchange for allowance.

## Care from pests

The most common organisms that you can expect to visit your containers are: frogs, mosquitoes, ants, algae, grasshoppers, caterpillars, etc. These would decrease the aesthetic factor of the plants and also can cause problems for you.

The problem of mosquitoes and frogs can be eliminated, by avoiding water stagnation. The pests can be removed by adding a limited amount of pesticides or insecticides to the soil. If you are planning to grow them organically, water the plants daily and clean off all the debris and other insects from the plants.

Caring for the container garden would not take much of your time. You might need to prune, re-plant and trim a few plants but, for most of them, all you need is to water them regularly. Removing dried parts and ensuring that the plants get enough sunlight and shades would make them grow faster and better.

## Three tips for a better garden

There are three main tips which would help you to have a better yield and good results.

a) Succession planting: plant more of the same kind after a week or two from planting the first batch. This would help you to continue harvesting, for a period of time. Moreover, even if a batch fails to grow, there will be another batch to take its place.

b) While planting the seeds, you should sow the seeds in the pot. After the seeds germinate into small saplings, remove most of the saplings in such a way that each sapling would have a considerable amount of space and water.

c) Increase the nutrients of the soil, by adding composite and other organic fertilizers.

## Care your plants from heavy winds

Heavy winds or hurricanes would destroy a lot of containers and make your garden, a mess. Here are a few tips to protect your plants from the heavy winds and hurricanes.

a) When the wind starts to blow hard, shift the containers to a safe place. Place it next to the walls, where the wind would be mostly blocked.

b) The best place would be the garage. It would be easy for you to transfer all the containers from the lawn to the garage.

c) If you have hanging baskets, remove them from the hook and place them on the floor.

d) Pick the fruits and vegetables from the plant after you place them in a safe place. Heavy parts of the body would lead to the breakage of the plant.

# CHAPTER 7: HOW TO MANAGE PLAGUE, DISEASE AND GET RID OF INSECTS

Photo by Walter** on Foter.com / CC BY-ND

Pest control is one of the more controversial topics with gardening because pest control is typically the reason that people are motivated to use chemicals and pesticides. When pests are left unchecked, they can cause damage to the plants and prevent the vegetables from growing. Or, if the vegetables are already growing, then the pests might start to eat the vegetables.

## Types of Garden Pests

Some types of pests are visible to the naked eye, and other pests cannot be seen by just looking at the plant. When it comes to pest control, it is best to be proactive to prevent the pests, because prevention is much easier than getting rid of pests that have already arrived.

Examples of garden pests include grubs, ants, fire ants, chiggers, fleas, ticks, beetles, weevils, flies, cats, rabbits, dogs, earwigs, fungi, deer, gnats, moles, slugs, snakes, and many more.

As this is a large subject in itself, we have a whole guide dedicated to it. Below are some of the more common problems and solutions.

## Organic Pest Control Options

Even though pests are inevitable, there are a few natural methods that can be used to get rid of the pests. Many people think that they need to reach for a chemical pest control product, but there is no reason to use those unnatural products when the natural solutions work just as well.

1. **Floating Plant Covers:** Lightweight translucent fabric can be placed over the plants to act as a literal barrier between the plants and the bugs. This fabric is not a long-term pest control solution, but it can be a great option if you need to protect your plant during critical growth periods, such as during seeding time or when a specific type of pest is most active.

Photo by Red Moon Sanctuary on Foter.com / CC BY

2. **Bacillus Thuringiensis:** This naturally occurring bacterium is found in the soil, and you can add more BT to repel many types of pests. There are several types of BT to choose from, and you need to select the type that is designed for the specific pest that you find in your garden.

3. **Insecticidal Soap:** A product with insecticidal soap contains compounds that are derived from the fat of certain animals, and the long-chain fatty acids within the fat can kill certain insects. When the insect comes in contact with the soap, it causes their skin to dissolve. The insect must come in contact with the liquid form of the soap; it does not work once the soap has dried. Also, be cautious, because insecticidal soap can cause burns on some plants.

4. **Sticky Traps:** A piece of material with a sticky surface is a great way to capture insects that are attracted to a certain color. When the insect flies into the trap, it gets stuck and cannot get free.

Photo by CarbonNYC [in SF!] on Foter.com / CC BY

5. **Pheromone Traps:** There are certain smells that are emitted by pests, in order to lure the opposite sex for mating. Scientists have found a way to duplicate some of these smells, and the pheromones cause the insects to be lured toward the trap. Keep in mind that these traps usually only catch the males, which means that the females are still running free in your garden. If you find that you are catching a lot of bugs in your pheromone trap, then it is a good sign that you should start implementing other pest control methods as well.

6. **Oil Spray:** When you spray a pest directly with horticultural oil, it can cause the insect to suffocate. This oil can also be applied to spores and pest eggs, to suffocate them before they hatch.

7. **Peppermint:** Put 20 to 30 drops of peppermint essential oil into a spray bottle and dilute it with water. Shake the bottle well before using, and spray it along the garden and on the plants. The peppermint is a repellant to many types of pests including insects and small rodents. It needs to be applied often because it will wash away after watering.

## Natural Fungicide Recipe

If you are struggling with fungicide problems, then there are a few natural remedies that you can try to get rid of the fungus. One of the easiest recipes uses apple cider vinegar:

Add 2 tablespoons of vinegar to a gallon of water. Put it in a spray bottle and spray the affected area every few days until the fungus problem is gone. Be careful, because the vinegar could potentially kill the plant, so you should use it very sparingly and only on the areas that are experiencing the fungus problems.

# WEED CONTROL

Controlling the weeds is an important part of maintaining your garden on an ongoing basis, because weed overgrowth can suffocate your plants. If you feel as though you are excelling at growing weeds, but your plants are suffering, then you might consider some of these natural weed-control options.

Keep in mind that the weeds are not as much of a problem once your vegetable plants are well established. You still need to make sure that you are weeding regularly, but the plants are at a lower risk of suffocating from the weeds once the plants have a solid root system in place.

## The Worst Vegetable Garden Weeds

There are two types of weeds that might pop up in your garden: annual and perennial weeds. The perennial weeds are the worst types because, if you do not get them under control, they will grow back every year. The weeds come up and then drop their seeds in the dirt, which remain dormant throughout the winter months and then start growing again in the spring. This problem occurs over and over again each year, especially if you do not pull the weeds before the seeds are dropped.

On the other hand, annual weeds can be difficult in their own way, because they grow and spread very quickly. Once they start to grow, it seems as though they take over the garden overnight.

Whether you are finding annual or perennial weeds, it is important that you take care of the weed problem as quickly as possible, in order to prevent bigger problems.

## Organic Weed Control Options

One of the easiest and most effective forms of weed control is mulching. When mulch is laid down between the plants, it blocks the weeds from popping up, and you do not have to weed very often.

Photo by La.Catholique on Foter.com / CC BY

Another natural weed control option is household vinegar. If the weeds are young, they will die when they are sprayed with vinegar, although it is not quite as effective on weeds that are well established in your garden. For the best results, you might need to apply the vinegar several times, in order to get enough acidity to kill the weed. Watch where you spray, because the vinegar may harm your vegetable plants as well.

Most household vinegar is 5% acetic acid. If you need something stronger, you can buy a bottle of 20% acetic acid vinegar. It works in the same way as the household vinegar, but it is usually faster and more effective. Be careful about using this vinegar on certain types of stone or concrete, because it may cause stains.

Corn gluten (this is not the same gluten that affects people with celiac disease) can be used to stop the weeds from growing in the first place, because it prevents the weed's seeds from germinating. The only problem with corn gluten is that it could potentially prevent the germination of your vegetable seeds as well, so it should not be used in a garden where you are starting the vegetables from seeds.

A long-handled "winged weeder" is a tool that can be found at any hardware or gardening store, and it makes weeding much easier. The truth is that it is very difficult to prevent weeds from growing, and one of the best things that you can do is to weed frequently in order to stop the weeds while they are young. This tool has a metal head that is in the shape of a "V," and it can be dragged along the top surface of the garden to uproot small weeds that may be growing. If you use this tool several times a week at the beginning of the growing season, it can help to slow the growth of the weeds in the season

# CHAPTER 8: CALENDAR

## January

First of all, at the beginning of the new year all residues of plants grown the previous year must be removed from the soil. Once this is done, if the climate allows it, you can start growing inside a greenhouse: summer cabbages, eggplants, tomatoes, peppers, radishes, celery, melons, watermelons, lettuces.

If you don't have a greenhouse, you can plant outdoors: white garlic, broad beans and peas.

## February

In this month you will sow the vegetables that you will harvest in spring. You must follow the sowing calendar which is influenced by the phases of the moon.

With the waning moon you will sow sheltered leafy greens and celery and plant chard, spinach and lettuce. On the other hand, carrots, radishes and peas are usually fertilized in the open air and herbs are grown under cover.

## March

Here you need to evaluate the type of climate present. In fact, if you sow too early there can be sudden drops in temperature or rains that can damage the whole crop.

In general, however, this month is the right one to proceed with sowing. As for the protected cultivation: watermelon, basil, artichokes, cabbage, cucumbers, endives, fennel, eggplants, peppers, tomatoes, leeks, celery, zucchini and herbs. While, outdoors: garden beets, carrots, chopped chicory, onions, lettuces, peas, parsley, turnips, radishes, arugula and spinach.

## April

During April you can plant: watermelons, asparagus, basil, chard and ribs, artichokes, thistles, carrots, cabbage, chicory, onions, endives, beans, green beans, fennel, salad, melons, eggplant, peppers, peas, parsley, radishes, arugula, celery, zucchini.

## May

Plants to sow are these: beans, green beans, peppers, eggplant, zucchini, Brussels sprouts, cucumbers, strawberries.

As we know, in May temperatures tend to rise, so it is advisable to water in the early morning hours and after sunset. This would serve to prevent excessive temperature changes from causing plants to wilt.

## June

This is the month of beets, basil, carrot, chard, cabbage, chicory, beans, lettuce, leek, parsley, radish, arugula, celery and zucchini.

In this month you need to pay attention to fungal diseases and insect attacks on already developed plants of tomatoes, eggplants and peppers. Also you should prepare supports for climbing plants.

## July and August

In these months you sow: basil, beets, carrots, cauliflower, chicory, onions, endive, fennel, beans, green beans, lettuce, parsley, radishes, turnips, arugula, valerian, zucchini.

Since these are the hottest months of the year, you should water regularly and keep an eye out for weeds and diseases that can attack the plant. In August you can iprepare the soil for transplanting chicory, cabbage, tomatoes and fennel.

## September

In this month you can sow beets, carrots, cabbage, chicory, endives, fennel, lettuce, parsley, turnips, radishes, arugula, spinach, valerian.

## October

We are in the fall and temperatures are getting colder and there are fewer varieties of plants suitable for this season. You can sow outdoors: chicory, fava beans, lettuce, parsley, radish, arugula, spinach, and valerian. Besides that you can also sow peas and plant onions.

You should always keep in mind the environmental conditions in which you are planting and how they are expected to change during the next season. Always remember to look at the forecast for next week and note when thunderstorms or high temperature rises are expected.

## November and December

During these months, beans, peas, radishes, spinach and valerian are sown outdoors. Lettuce, green chicory, arugula are grown in small greenhouses or under glass. In addition, throughout the month of November and until the first fortnight of December, you can still plant peas and bulbs of onion and garlic.

These are the general guidelines on managing a vegetable garden. As we have just seen, there are better times to plant and better times to harvest. We have also seen that planting times vary depending on the type of vegetable.

I return to reiterate that these are general principles and that, therefore, can also be applied to gardening in containers.

# CHAPTER 9 : WHEN TO PLANT?

We repeat, to answer this question the determining factor is what you are planting. For example, Tomatoes prefer a warmer climate than lettuce. When you're looking for information about a particular vegetable, you don't have to limit yourself to just the ideal temperature. If you go to your local garden store, remember to ask what the maximum and minimum temperature is that the plant can handle. Most plants should be planted in the spring. In fact, plants that can withstand lower temperatures are planted in early spring; those that prefer warmer temperatures are planted in late spring. As a result, almost all plants are ready for harvest in the summer. Remember to pay attention to two key details when both planting and harvesting. First, you need to know the time of the last frost of the winter season. The general rule of thumb is that you don't plant anything before this date. If you start your plants indoors, and later transport the container with the seedlings outside, then you will need to plant the seeds about three weeks before the last expected frost. So, if you are growing fruits, vegetables or herbs for harvest, then you will need to identify when the first frost of the winter season is. Many harvestable plants will not withstand the frost and will die; so you will need to harvest them before this time.

The other element to watch out for is the soil temperature. This temperature should be between 60F and 70F. However there are exceptions, as there are many whose seeds will germinate even better at a lower temperature, but for the most part you will need 60F if you want the seeds to germinate properly.

I recommend getting a soil thermometer and monitoring the soil temperature every day. If you take a look at the weather every day, these two habits together will help you understand what weather factors affect soil temperature and in time you will be able to judge just by looking at the weather. You should know, however, that even gardeners who have mastered this skill check the soil temperature before planting. It always pays to be sure when deciding to plant.

Also, whether you are planting seeds or transplanting seedlings, you should not put your containers outside when it is too windy or raining. Rain can unfortunately affect the health of your plants. You need to keep the soil dry when you plant and then water afterwards. The wind could blow the seeds away or damage the seedlings. In these cases, you need to strengthen your seedlings before planting them to prevent the strong wind from damaging them.

So far we have talked about when to plant as only happening once a season. It is true, if you are growing tomatoes, peppers or eggplant, which are crops that take a long time to ripen, in fact in this case you will plant once a season. But if you are growing lettuce for example, then you could harvest and plant several times a season. Vegetables like lettuce can be harvested early and still enjoyed as microgreens. You could, even, plant them up to three times from the last frost.

# CHAPTER 10: HARVESTING STAGE

Photo by Percita on Foter.com / CC BY-SA

Harvest time is the fun part! Now you get to pluck the fruits and vegetables from your garden and enjoy them. If you have a small garden, you shouldn't have too much trouble keeping up with your harvest, but if you have chosen to go with a much larger garden, then you might have trouble keeping up with the harvest. This problem can be solved by picking the fruits and vegetables as soon as they are ripe. Just keep in mind that this encourages the plant to produce even more fruit and vegetables, which isn't a bad thing at all.

Remember, some vegetables are actually at their peak when they are smaller than you'd expect. This isn't the case with everything, but with zucchini, for example, you should pick them before they get much longer than six or seven inches. If you wait until they get larger than that, you will notice that they will get a lot tougher. Of course, you can still use these tougher zucchinis for making zucchini bread or cookies if you grate them up first.

When you are ready to harvest, make sure that you check your seed packet so you know what the ripe fruit should be like. You should have saved your seed packets from earlier. If not, then you may be able to go on the internet and find out when you should pick most of your fruits and vegetables. Remember, some fruits and vegetables are bred specifically to be smaller or larger. Watermelon is a good example. You can find watermelon seeds that are best when the fruit is very small, and others will tell you to wait until the fruit has reached a weight of 25-30 pounds before you harvest it.

You also want to make sure that you look out for bad fruit signs. If you look out for yellow leaves or fruit that has become rotten, you can remove these parts and keep it from spreading to another part of the plant. Also, trimming off the parts of the plant that are not any good allows the plant to put its energy into growing the parts that are good.

There are hundreds of fruits and vegetables out there to choose from. Here are some additional harvest instructions for some of the most common fruits and vegetables often chosen by first-time gardeners.

**Herbs:** One of the things that you can do with herbs is to prune them regularly. This allows the herb plant to continue to produce more of the stems and leafy parts, which are the parts that we use. It will also keep them from getting to full bloom which changes the flavor of the herb. If you have more thyme or oregano, you can dry them in a paper bag. If you are growing basil, you need to continually pinch it to keep it bushy.

**Tomatoes:** There are so many different kinds of tomatoes out there that it can be difficult to instruct you on pruning your tomato vine in a way that will work for every type of tomato plant. They range in size from very tiny to extremely large, and while we mostly think of tomatoes as red fruit, they can actually come in yellow, green, orange, or even striped colors. You can look at your seed packet or check the internet for instructions on your specific variety. However, here is some instruction that will work for just about any variety of tomato that you happen to be raising.

Most of the time, you can tell that a tomato is ready for picking when you can easily pluck it from the stem. If the tomato resists being picked, then you might want to leave it on the plant for a little longer. However, you can pick tomatoes a little bit early if you want, or if you accidentally pick a tomato that isn't yet ripe, don't worry, because tomatoes are fruits that will ripen a little bit after they are picked. However, the best tasting tomatoes are allowed to ripen on the vine.

After some time dealing with your specific variety of tomato, you will learn when it is the best time to pick your fruit and when you should wait a little bit longer. Don't be afraid of trial and error. That's how the best gardeners become so good at growing fruit and vegetables that taste great.

There are two different types of tomatoes. Some tomatoes are known as determinate vines, meaning that they will produce a certain amount of fruit for a period of weeks, and then they will stop. However, indeterminate vines will continue to produce fruit constantly until they have been killed by the winter frost. If you know that you are going to have a frost coming up, it is a good idea to pick your tomatoes, even if they are green, about a week or so before the frost comes. They will still continue to ripen somewhat if you store them at room temperature. You should wrap each tomato in a paper so that they don't touch each other while they are ripening. If you'd like, you can use your green ones to make fried green tomatoes, a tasty treat.

**Peppers:** You can tell very easily whether a pepper is ready to be picked or not by its color, and you can leave them on the vine longer for a different flavor. Depending upon what variety of peppers you have, they will be ripe when they have reached full size, but are still green. However, if you leave them to change color to orange, yellow, brown or red, you will notice a deeper flavor. They will also be less crisp if you allow them to ripen further.

As for hot peppers, they work almost exactly the same way, except that the longer that you leave them on the vine the hotter they will get. You can decide for yourself whether to pick your peppers when they are green, or if you want to wait longer for them to ripen further and change the flavor.

**Lettuce:** Lettuce is a popular plant to grow, but it is also rather tricky to pick. You want to pick your lettuce before the leaves get bitter. That means that you have to pick your lettuce before it develops a flower stalk. You can pick lettuce when the leaves are very young, and only about five inches long. This works the same with many other greens as well. You can remove the longer leaves from the plant with your garden shears and you'll be able to harvest the plant several times before the heat of the summer ruins the plant. There are some varieties of lettuce that are resistant to developing the flower stalk. You can reduce this somewhat by shading your lettuce from the intense heat.

**Green Beans:** There are a couple of things to keep in mind when you are harvesting green beans. First, you want to pick them when they are a bit smaller than the maximum size that they will get. This will, of course, come with experience, or you might want to check your seed packet or look on the internet to find out how big they are going to get. The reason for this is, you want to pick the beans when they are soft and tender, when the seeds haven't yet matured. If you pick them when they reach their maximum size, the seeds and the pod will become hard.

**Peas:** Learning when it is time to harvest peas is rather simple. You just need to open one of the pea pods and check to see if the seeds are starting to swell. The peas should be round, but not hard. Instead, they should be soft and tender. The best way to pick your peas is right before you are ready to eat them.

**Cantaloupe and Honeydew Melon:** Melons are a little more complex to test. There are a couple of things that you can do to find out if the melon is ready to be picked or not, but it does require some practice. Method one is to smell the melon and see if the scent is sweet or not. You can also thump the melon and see if it sounds dull and hollow. If so, then it is time to pick the melon. You do want to make sure that you don't pull the melon off of the stem, because you can damage the melon which will make it rot quickly. Instead, take your gardening shears and cut the melon stem off. Then, let it ripen for another couple of days at room temperature before you eat it.

**Watermelon:** Watermelon is ripe when the spot on the ground where the melon is sitting turns a yellow color. When the ground is white or green, the melon is not ready. You can test the rind of the watermelon with your fingernail to see how tough the rind is. If it is too soft, it is not yet ripe. Watermelon, depending upon the variety that you are growing, can be tricky. You may simply have to cut open a watermelon and check and see if it is ripe yet. If it is, then you are likely able to pick the rest of the crop.

**Cucumbers:** These are always a favorite of a first-time farmer. Finding out if cucumbers are ready to be picked is as simple as checking the back of your seed packet to find out how big they are supposed to get. However, cucumbers can be picked at varying times depending upon what you are going to use them for.

**Sweet Corn:** This is another tricky one. You have to check your sweet corn carefully because once you have picked the ear, the sweetness will begin to fade. That means that you shouldn't pick your corn until you are ready to use it for that meal. This literally means, start boiling your pot of water to cook the corn, and then go out and pick the ears that you want. It is a simple matter, however, to tell whether they are ready to be picked. You will be able to feel, full plump and rounded kernels of corn that are beneath the husk and the silk at the top of the corn is starting to dry out. If you need additional verification, then squeeze one of the kernels of corn. It should exude a milky sap.

**Rooted Vegetables:** Finally, let's cover some basics about rooted veggies. Of course, you are going to have to use this information in accordance with whatever it says on your seed packet about when the vegetables are ready. You can pull up one of the root vegetables gently from the ground (loosen the soil if you need to) and check to see if they are ready. Many rooted vegetables are tastier when they are younger, so you can pick them even if they haven't reached full maturity.

# CHAPTER 11: VERTICAL GARDENING

Vertical gardening is the concept of growing plants upwards. Earlier I talked about growing plants such as cucumbers vertically, which basically means growing them up a trellis or something similar but there is a lot more you can do than just that.

Vertical gardens can become a work of art and have become popular in cities and built-up areas where they make use of walls that are otherwise bare. These are usually made up of evergreen plants and flowers to brighten up an otherwise drab city.

However, at home, you can use any wall or fence and turn it into a productive vegetable garden. Before you do anything though you need to ensure that your wall/fence is sturdy enough and will be able to support the weight of the containers.

If it is then you need to determine what containers you are going to use. You can buy specific container systems for vertical gardens, some of which are actually freestanding;

Photo by vastateparksstaff on Foter.com / CC BY

though you can use pretty much any container, you must consider the weight of the container plus the soil. For most vertical gardens, you will use lightweight plastic pots and fix them securely to the wall, making sure drainage holes are in place first. Do not use heavy metal or stone containers as they will end up damaging the wall due to their weight.

Many of the wall-mounted systems consist of a number of pockets that you can plant up with herbs or vegetables. Most of these are not suitable for larger plants but they are great for growing all sorts of different plants. Ican recommend these systems as they are easy to fix to your wall and will last 3 to 5 years or sometimes longer depending on the weather conditions where you live.

Alternatively, you can make your own vertical garden from bought containers or you can make support from metal and use large soda bottles. Simply lay them on their side and cut a hole in the top for the soil and plant. Punch some drainage holes, put the lid back on and you have a container that you can use for your vertical garden. If you want to keep the budget to a minimum then there are plenty of items you can reuse and fix to your wall to grow plants in.

One thing that you must consider is drainage as it is, as you know, very important. You not only need to ensure that there are sufficient drainage holes in your container but you need to think where the excess water will go. Ifit is going to drip down on to the street or a neighbor then you may have a problem! Plan for where excess water will go so it doesn't cause a nuisance. Another major consideration is access. Itis all well and good having a vertical garden up the entire side of your house but if you can't reach your plants to water, maintain and harvest them then you are going to have issues. An irrigation system can make watering easier but you will still need to be able to get to your plants to harvest your crops.

Vertical gardens are by far one of the best ways for you to maximize your growth potential in a small area. Ifyou live in a built-up area or have limited space then vertical gardening can significantly increase the amount of space available to you and maximize your yield.

# CHAPTER 12: BALCONY VEGETABLE GARDEN

**THE LOCATION**

Compared to the garden or vegetable garden, the balcony is much more constrained. The choice of plants to sow also depends on this factor.

To give an example, if you grow your strawberries on a balcony where the sun shines all day long, you can be sure that the sun will burn them before you can harvest them.

So, you need to consider the location of your balcony when deciding on the type of plants to plant.

By looking at your balcony, you need to realize where the sun rises and sets. If you need some shade, you could plant ivy or use a tarp as a cover.

So, when creating your balcony vegetable garden you will need to be concerned about knowing exactly how much sun and shade and also how much heat your vegetable garden has.

**CREATE THE LAYERS FOR YOUR GROWING MEDIUM**

First, you need to get yourself a saucer.

The saucer will allow you to retain water and will also keep your balcony clean. In addition, your plants will receive more humidification because of the particular type of climate on your balcony.

I recommend putting a layer of either pebbles or expanded clay in the bottom of your pot. You need to do this to facilitate water drainage so that your roots don't rot.

Once you have done this, place the pebbles or clay evenly.

Now it's time to add the potting soil.

Unfortunately, many people settle for poor quality potting soil. The poorer the potting soil, the less nutrients the plants will have available to them and consequently there is a risk that they will get sick and bear less fruit.

So my advice is to buy potting soil. Before buying it, read the label on the package to see what the potting soil contains. A good potting soil consists of compost and peat, which is very rich in nutrients.

However, if you already have a tank with potting soil, you will need to regenerate that potting soil. I still recommend replacing the potting soil with new soil at least every two years. If you have decided to reactivate the potting soil, you will need to remove 1/3 of the old soil and add compost.

Going back to the pot filling stage, pour the potting soil over the layer of pebbles or clay. In every pot you buy there is always a frame; you must try not to go over the frame.

I recommend buying pots with rigid rods in them. These rods are used to hold the pot firmly in place so that when you fill it with soil, it does not deform.

## CHOOSING A POT

The choice of the pot should be made in relation to the size of the plant once it has become an adult and especially to the size of its roots.

For example, if the container is too small, there will not be enough soil for the plant's nourishment and the roots will be poorly sheltered.

In general, trays should not be lower than 8 inches, while shrub trays should be at least 15-20 inches deep.

As mentioned at the beginning of this book, it is important that the pots have holes in the bottom for water drainage.

Let's talk about the materials.

Terracotta, given its porosity, allows oxygen to circulate well, allowing the roots to breathe. Terracotta pots are suitable for plants that need a dry substrate because they allow moisture to evaporate quickly.

Always remember that new pots should be moistened before use.

Plastic pots, on the other hand, are less breathable and retain more moisture, but tend to overheat during the summer.

Wood is also porous and does not get particularly hot in the sun, thus retaining moisture in the potting soil. However, wood does have a tendency to rot over time.

# CHAPTER 13: FERTILIZING MY VEGETABLES

When you frequently water your plants, the nutrients in the soil normally leach out. Fertilizers can supply the soil and plant with the nutrients they need, especially when you have to supply a lot of water to your containers. Fertilizers are food for plants, and they provide your garden plants with the nutrients they need to survive and grow.

There are two kinds of fertilizers—inorganic and organic. Inorganic fertilizers deliver food to your plants quickly whereas organic ones do this slowly. Organic fertilizers are created from living organisms and, as such, bring fungi and bacteria to your soil, as well as texture—inorganic does not. Some of the organic types of fertilizers consist of worm manure, compost, and seaweed. Be sure to purchase these from a reputable dealer before adding to your containers.

Inorganic fertilizers are chemical additives. Usually available in two forms—liquids and solids—these supply ingredients like potassium, calcium, zinc, nitrogen, and other important nutrients to your plants. Solid fertilizers tend to release nutrients slowly over time while liquids feed your plants much quicker.

## Choose the Right Fertilizers

Because your plants cannot obtain the nutrients they might otherwise get from the natural environment, you need to provide adequate nutrition to your plants by choosing the right fertilizer.

A slow-release fertilizer normally supplies the plant with nutrients for 60 to 120 days. It works by releasing nutrients once it comes in contact with water. This means that every time you water your plant, you are automatically fertilizing it.

You can assist the efficiency of the slow-release fertilizer by applying a water-soluble fertilizer as well. This product will take care of delivering the nutrients to the roots of your plants. A water-soluble fertilizer is normally dissolved in water and poured into the container.

There are also spray water-soluble fertilizers you can use to aid stressed plants. You can cut the damaged parts of the plants and spray the fertilizer. This will allow the nutrients to go directly into the plant and can result in the plant's dramatic growth and renewal.

One of the secrets in feeding your containerized plants is to use controlled-release granular fertilizer. You can use this when you plant your plants or sprinkle it over the soil's surface. Controlled-release fertilizers can provide the nutritional needs of your plants even without the use of soluble fertilizers. Choose a product that contains appropriate amounts of potassium, phosphorus and nitrogen.

You may want to consider using organic fertilizers as these can significantly help increase the plant's protection from pests. This type of fertilizer can also make your vegetables more nutritious, flavorful and aromatic.

## Know the Signs of the Plant's Nutritional Deficiencies and How to Fertilize

Photo by Ivan Radic on Foter.com / CC BY

Certain symptoms normally appear when a plant experiences nutritional deficiency. These symptoms are your plant's way of communicating to you what it needs. Knowing about these symptoms will also help you understand and determine what the best fertilizers for your plants are. Look at the details below to see how certain nutritional deficiencies manifest themselves in the plant's appearance:

- Calcium deficiency – This deficiency will display symptoms such as leaf discoloration and brown spots.

- Nitrogen and sulfur deficiency – Stunted plant growth and its older leaves will appear lighter than the young leaves.

- Phosphorus deficiency – This condition also exhibits discoloration symptoms. Most often, the top side of the old leaves will turn dark green and the bottom part turns red.

- Potassium deficiency – This impedes water absorption in plants and the growth of new tissues. The plant normally dies when it suffers from this deficiency.

If containerized plants are not given time-release fertilizer, you will need to feed them once every two weeks with a water-soluble fertilizer. During midway through the growing season, you can treat your crops with liquid fertilizer about once a week. This is essential for your plants during this time because this is normally when they start producing their fruit.

If you are raising root vegetables, feed them with fertilizers that are rich in phosphorus. However, if you are growing leaf vegetables, use nitrogen-rich fertilizers. When you are watering your plants daily, you need to provide your vegetables with liquid fertilizer once a week, especially when the weather is hot or dry. You can apply the liquid fertilizer every other week if you don't irrigate frequently or when the weather is cool. Always remember to follow the instructions provided on the fertilizer's label.

## Things You Should Not Do When Fertilizing

1. You should not sprinkle too much granular fertilizer in the soil because this can cause the burning of your plants.

2. Avoid fertilizing plants that are dried, sick or wilted. Instead, water them and then treat them with a water-soluble fertilizer. Only use this treatment once you see the plants are well watered and have recovered.

3. Avoid overfeeding your plants because it will not speed up their growth. When you apply amounts of fertilizer that are more than the suggested dosage, or when you use it longer than recommended, it can be fatal to your plants.

# CHAPTER 14: WATERING

Watering needs are extremely important for any kind of plant whether you are growing vegetables, fruits, flowers, or just ornamental houseplants. However, when it comes to container gardening, water is another factor that needs special consideration and planning for your plants to survive and thrive. Since containers don't have the natural drainage system your plants would have if planted in the ground, figuring out the water amount and frequency is vital to their growth. You don't want to over-water or under-water – both have disastrous consequences for a container garden. The water your plants need can vary significantly according to the location (indoors or outdoors), environment (weather and temperature), and specific plant requirements.

**Location** – Whether your plants are in a controlled location (indoors) or exposed to seasonal temperatures (outdoors) will determine how often they need to be watered. In general, container plants growing outside will usually require daily watering and sometimes twice daily during hot weather seasons. Plants outside are more vulnerable to death by under-watering while plants indoors can easily be over-watered and drown.

**Environment** – If your container garden is outside and exposed to the elements, most likely it will require extra water during the hottest parts of the year. While heat can help the plants grow faster, it also dries out the soil faster making daily watering essential. The hotter weather can also be a bigger issue for plants indoors if you don't have an air conditioner and a controlled temperature setting inside. Windy weather outside can also dry soil faster, so if you live in an area that usually deals with a lot of wind, you need to monitor the water needs of your plants closely.

**Plant Requirements** – How much water a plant needs also depends on its optimal growing needs. Some plants grow better if they dry out completely between watering while others grow best if the soil is always damp. This characteristic varies from plant to plant, and you should be able to find the soil recommendation on the seed label or store packaging material...and of course, such specific information is easily found online just by searching for the best growing environment for whatever plants you're trying to grow.

## Self-Watering & Vacation-Watering Methods

While container gardening is indeed a relatively easy way to grow plants and edibles, water needs can be a bit challenging to meet if you are super busy or go on vacation while your plants are growing. But you don't have to let watering stop you from enjoying time away from home because there are some inexpensive ways you can provide adequate water to your plants without having to water them in person every day.

# **Water Bottle Method**

You know those millions of empty plastic water and soda bottles that wind up in landfills and polluting the environment around the world? Well, you can use them to help yourself, your plants, and the planet all at the same time! Watering your plants with bottles is surprisingly simple but quite effective. All you have to do is place some small rocks in the bottom of the bottle (to stabilize it in case of wind gusts), poke some holes in it, fill with water, and place in the container right next to your plant. The water will slowly trickle out and provide your plant with the hydration it needs to both survive and thrive. You will need to do a little experimenting to see how many holes you need to poke in the bottle to determine how fast the water needs to drain out, but it is worth the effort. If you are going to be away from home for a few days, the bigger the bottle the better – even empty milk jugs can do the trick, and you will enjoy helping your plants and the environment at the same time.

## Plastic Baggie Method

This method works similarly to the way the plastic bottle method works, and it is one more way to use items that would otherwise wind up in a landfill. Gently used zipper-type bags can be filled with water and placed on the soil next to your container plant. There needs to be at least 2-3 tiny holes in the plastic bag so water can leak out and hydrate your plant, and voila! You've got a self-watering plant. One benefit this method holds above the bottle method is baggies can be molded to fit in between plants in the same pot or can fit in other tight places where a bottle won't fit.

## Clay Pot Method

Another ingenious trick to take some of the work out of watering your plants sufficiently is by using clay pots to provide that continuous moisture your plants need to survive. This method calls for unglazed clay pots that have their drainage holes sealed with clay, putty, or even duct tape. Simply bury the pot next to your plant so the rim of the pot is level with the soil surface in your container. Fill the pot with water that will gradually be absorbed as the soil dries out thus watering the plant without any additional work necessary until the clay pot is empty.

Photo by steveilott on Foter.com / CC BY

# CHAPTER 15: CHOOSE THE SEEDS OR STARTER PLANTS

Whether you decide to grow from organic seeds or starter plants, you want to select the veggies, herbs and fruits you like best and plant the varieties that thrive best in your climate.

Think of types of products that are hard to find, expensive to buy, but easy to grow—like herbs, salad greens, peppers, and broccoli. Consider the number and style of containers you have listed on your sun map. A good nursery will have organic seeds and organic starter plants from local companies, along with experts that can offer advice on growing them.

Master Gardeners can be found at the local community garden, garden club, or library, who are happy to tell you where to get organic starter plants—and maybe even share seeds.

There are so many choices that it's important (and fun) to study seed catalogs, websites, and seed packets for detailed growing information.

## Organic Seeds

A miracle starts with the tiny seed! Conventional seeds and starter plants take several years of organic growth to be considered organic. Because some seeds and starter plants have been genetically modified to include a poison in their DNA, look for the non-GMO, certified organic label on the plant marker or seed package, which will also indicate if it is locally grown.

Seeds need oxygen in the soil, enough water and warmth to sprout. The seed packet tells what season to sow those seeds, when the plants will be ready for harvest, the characteristics of each plant and the growing requirements—like how much space it needs, sun or shade, heat tolerance, soil moisture and planting depth.

Seeds can be sowed directly into the soil, sowed in a wet paper towel, sowed in plastic trays with multiple small compartments, or sowed in a replantable pot like coconut coir. Many seeds can be planted a one-half inch deep in organic vegetable potting soil right in the containers they will occupy. However, every plant has a unique seed with specific needs—celery prefers foot-deep trenches—and the packet lists these sprouting requirements and indicates the number of days before the seeds sprout.

Because garden pests love tender young sprouts, it is best to sprout seeds indoors—they also sprout faster inside. Here are three methods to sprout indoors:

(1) Place the seeds on half of a damp paper towel, fold the towel over the seeds, and place it in a labeled plastic sandwich bag in a safe warm spot.

(2) Place two or three seeds in each of the pockets of a plastic tray filled with potting soil to the depth indicated on the seed packet.

(3) Place the seeds in moist potting soil in plantable organic coconut coir pots and sprout indoors for the first week or two.

Keep the growing seeds indoors in a warm dark place until they sprout and then move them to a sunny window. When seedlings are grown in individual plug trays or plantable fiber pots, you can know exactly which seeds have germinated and which have not and choose the strongest and biggest sprouts—and start more seeds if necessary.

## Transplanting Organic Starter Plants

When seedlings are about two inches tall, they need to be placed outdoors in a warm sheltered place to allow them to acclimatize to the outside conditions and temperatures before planting. At four or five inches tall, seedlings are less vulnerable to cutworms, rabbits, and birds and can be transplanted.

If you have purchased your organic veggie plants at the garden center, check the plant marker on the starter plant to see if it is grown locally and will do well in your area. Check your sun map to find the location you have marked for that plant. Fill the chosen container with moist organic potting soil and make a cavity for the plant in the soil where it has room to grow. Carefully remove the plant from the plastic pot, easing the root ball into the cavity, and cover it with extra soil.

To avoid root disturbance, seedlings sowed in replantable pots can be placed straight into the soil of the chosen container (properly-sized for the fully-grown plant). The organic pot quickly rots, allowing the roots to penetrate the soil, and earthworms love to eat coconut coir.

NOTE: Mark each container with plant labels that you have made or bought to know which veggies are planted where.

## Heirloom Seed Saving

The wonder of organic container gardening continues when you harvest the seeds from the best plants to replant the next year or swap seeds with fellow gardeners. Seed-saving is the work of organic home gardeners and is crucial to saving heirloom veggies, as 94% of vintage open-pollinated fruit and vegetable varieties have vanished in the last century. Thomas Jefferson's heirloom vegetable garden at Monticello survives today as a lasting monument to his seed-saving efforts.

Gardening can be spiritual as you contemplate the tiny apple seed becoming a full-grown tree. You can engage all your senses in gardening, tuning into the essence of life and watching the cycle of birth, growth and death—the birth of the seed into the plant; growth of vegetable or fruit; eventual death (and eventual composting) of the plant itself.

*"The Indian made an effort to know of spiritual things from his own observations of nature because all truth can be found in Nature."*
—Eli Gatoga, Cherokee (1914-1983)

## Susan Sundell, Master Gardener, President of Las Flores Community Garden

Blossoming under the leadership of Susan Sundell, the Las Flores Community Garden of Thousand Oaks, California, has become the largest community garden in Ventura County—and the only one with a Kids' Garden.

Sundell has worked with the Parks and Recreation Department, who governs the garden, and has received grants from various businesses to bring the very best amenities, equipment, and supplies to create an inspiring, productive, and beautiful garden. The new greenhouse has a reverse-osmosis water-filtration system with a mist sprayer and a table for seed sowing. The lovely new pergola with seating that converts to picnic tables holds member meetings, monthly public lectures, and garden feasts. The new shed for the Kids' Garden and the large main garden shed is filled with tools and supplies for members to use. The herbs from the herb garden plot and the fruit from the recently planted fruit trees along the fence are shared by the entire community—any surplus fruit is donated to local food banks, along with surplus produce from the garden's members.

## Life begins the day you start a garden. . .

A garden is a friend you can visit any time.

*"There are so many benefits of growing herbs, fruits, and veggies in a community garden, because there are so many resources and opportunities with various members. With so many knowledgeable and experienced gardeners readily willing to share, every day in a community garden is an education," said Sundell. "Our community garden is all organic because we gardeners want to provide the best*

*products to our families and friends. Organic gardening promises to be herbicide and pesticide-free and is the best choice."*

Sundell continued, *"I grew every vegetable possible in seven-gallon containers at home until I joined a community garden.*

*Due to physical limitations, I have two-foot-high raised beds. Raised beds allow me plenty of room to grow everything from seed, which is my passion. I enjoy growing in containers and raised beds that can be filled with the best organic soil and compost in a protected environment. I still grow in containers at home due to our drought conditions, and it amazes me how much produce can come from a few containers."*

# CHAPTER 16: TYPES OF COMPOST BIN

There are many styles and types of composters to choose from. They can vary by shape, material, size and mechanical action. There's not really a right or wrong answer when choosing a composter -- it's all about what works best for you and your yard. Check out this short guide to various types of composters and see what you like best!

## 1. Compost Piles

Okay, so it's pretty obvious that a compost pile isn't really a bin. But "no bin" is also an option. Master gardeners and master composters often swear that building a big 3-foot-by-3-foot pile is the most effective way to compost. And they might be right. It is also the cheapest option, since all you need to do is pick a spot and start piling.

But there are some serious potential drawbacks to composting in a pile instead of using a bin:

First, it might not be allowed if you live in town. Some cities don't allow big compost piles, because they can attract rats, raccoons, squirrels and other pests that use the pile as food or shelter. If you're mostly composting yard waste and no kitchen scraps, then this isn't as big of an issue. But if you are putting kitchen scraps in your pile, then you are looking for trouble. Master gardeners will tell you to bury the kitchen scraps at the bottom of the pile, under the yard waste, and that is indeed your best hope to keep the pests away.

Second, are you ready to get out there with a pitchfork to turn your giant pile? A big pile is a great way to get your compost nice and hot. But a big pile also needs to get mixed up and aerated, and that means pitchfork time! You could choose not to turn it, but that means 6-12 months before the pile is finished.

Third, do you like your neighbors? They might not like you if you have a large, ugly compost pile going next door, where they can see it. And if you start attracting rats and squirrels, you can bet that they probably won't be inviting you to the next block party.

If you do go with the pile method, avoid making it too big. Not only is it unmanageable, but some say that piles over 10 square feet have the potential to spontaneously combust!

## 2. Compost Pits or Trenches

Photo by Sustainable sanitation on Foter.com / CC BY

Once again, a pit or a trench isn't a bin, but it's another low-cost option.

It's a simple concept that is usually used with the batch composting method. You dig a pit or a trench in an area where you wish to start a garden, throw in all your materials, and then cover them with dirt. The materials begin to rot and break down underground.

That in turn attracts earthworms that help out with the process. In one labor-intensive step, you add a huge amount of rich organic material into your soil, improving it greatly.

Another advantage of using a compost pit or trench is that you can safely compost things that aren't advisable when composting above ground. You can throw in meat, bones and dog poop, no problem. However, if you plan on planting a food crop in that spot, continue to avoid those things.

The downside is that you have to have all of your materials ready to compost at once. So, it's not a good method for composting your kitchen scraps regularly. But it works well with garden debris at the end of a gardening season, or with leaves in the fall.

If you have a patch of dirt where nothing really grows, digging it out and turning it into a compost trench or pit can help improve the quality of soil in that area and get things growing.

While the rewards are great, few people do this type of composting, because digging trenches is not easy! In this case, a backhoe is man's best friend.

## 3. Wire Composters

Photo by nancybeetoo on Foter.com / CC BY

Wire bins are nice because they provide really good airflow for the materials inside the composter. Those wire sides let in the sun, the rain, and air, which all help the composting process. However, they also clearly display the contents of the bin itself. So, if you have picky neighbors, a wire bin might cause objections. Wire bins can also susceptible to pests if you add a lot of kitchen scraps, so it might be a better idea to use them for garden debris, grass clippings and leaves instead.

If you're handy, you may want to save some money and build your own wire bin. However, whether you decide to build it or buy it, go for a thick wire gauge rather than just the cheapest chicken wire you can find. Chicken wire doesn't last very long, and it doesn't hold its shape very well.

Wire bins come in both rectangular and round shapes. I like the Lewis Lifetime Wire Compost Bin, which is made from PVC-coated 12-gauge steel wire -- the same material as lobster cages. If it can sit under the ocean for extended periods of time, think about how long it will last in your yard. This bin also has the option of a lid on top, which helps keep animals out.

## 4. Wood Composters

Photo by andy_carter on Foter.com / CC BY

Wood compost bins are great because you can build them BIG! There are only a few commercial wood composters on the market -- most are DIY. Some feel wood bins are more attractive and natural-looking than plastic bins. They blend with the landscape and at the same time hide what's inside better than wire bins. A drawback is that wood bins tend to deteriorate pretty quickly.

Important note: If you build your own, don't use railroad ties! They are impregnated with toxic chemicals that can leech into your compost. And stay away from arsenic-treated wood. The lumber industry has moved away from using arsenic in the past few years, but any old pressure-treated lumber you have lying around was probably treated with arsenic. You don't want to poison your plants instead of strengthening them!

## 5. Plastic Composters

Photo by <ins>Steven Parker</ins> on <ins>Foter.com</ins> / <ins>CC BY</ins>

Plastic bins can come in round and rectangular shapes, or just about any other shape you can think (pig anyone?), because hey, it's plastic!

Plastic bins are often a good choice because they are sturdy, and they are usually designed to keep the materials in your bin well-insulated! Plastic composters can come with or without lids. Unlike wood, plastic will last for many years without beginning to rot and wear out.

Look for one with a top that's easy to open and close, so it's easy for you to keep adding materials to it. And be sure the top secures firmly, so it doesn't blow away in the wind.

And look for recycled plastic! You're recycling yard and food waste into compost, so doesn't it make sense to use recycled plastic to do it?

The cool thing about round compost bins is that they don't have corners. In a square or rectangular bin, it's usually the materials in the corners of the bin that take the longest to break down, because they are furthest away from the hot center of the bin. No corners in a round bin! The downside is that you can't put them flat up against a wall, which means more weed-eating around the back if you have the bin sitting on your lawn.

I use a rectangular-shaped plastic bin that has a removable lid, and a door at the bottom that slides open, so I can remove finished compost without emptying the entire bin.

## 6. Compost Tumblers (Tumbling Compost Bins)

Photo by MizGingerSnaps on Foter.com / CC BY-SA

Compost tumblers are suspended from a central axis so that they can be rotated. They are great because they make it easier to keep your compost well-mixed and aerated. Instead of using a pitchfork or a compost-aerating tool, you simply tumble the composter to stir up the contents.

Another benefit of tumbling composters is that they kept the compost up off the ground and closed off, away from pests.

And even better, they often work quickly. Some tumbling composter manufacturers claim that you can have finished compost in as little as two weeks!

So, what's not to like about tumbling compost bins? Like with everything else in life, there are a few trade-offs. Compost tumblers are typically more expensive than non-tumbling composters. And they usually have a smaller capacity than compost bins that sit on the ground. So, if you have a huge amount of yard waste and leaves to deal with, you'll probably fill up your tumbler before you run out of materials. To make up for this, some people keep several tumblers going at once, or they combine a tumbler with a regular bin.

I keep a tumbler near my back porch and use it primarily for kitchen scraps.

## 7. Multi-Stage Composters

A multi-stage compost bin is exactly what it sounds like. It's a bin that has different compartments that hold the compost in various stages as it breaks down. Typically, the first stage is where you'll throw in fresh materials like vegetable scraps. They'll dry out a little bit and rot until they are mostly unrecognizable. At that point, you move the material into the second stage, where it continues to break down. The third stage is where it goes last, and where it turns into finished compost that you can take out and use.

If you don't have a multi-stage compost bin, you can still use this method by using more than one compost bin. It's the same concept, except that you move the material from one bin to another, instead of just from one section to another. Most experienced composters use two bins. The first bin for the freshest material, and the second bin for the material that has already started breaking down, but still need to finish up. Empty the second bin when the compost is ready. At that point, you can start filling the second bin with new material and leave the first bin to finish up undisturbed.

# 8. Indoor Compost Bins

Photo by UCI Sustainability on Foter.com / CC BY-ND

What? You can compost indoors? Yes, you can.

Most indoor composters are designed to compost just kitchen scraps, and not yard waste. (Who has room for 10 bags of leaves in the house, right?)

One type of indoor compost bin is an anaerobic composter, which means no air. Regular compost breaks down with bacteria that like oxygen, but anaerobic bins break down materials with bacteria that don't like oxygen. You typically add your scraps into a sealed bin that doesn't let any air inside, and then you add material like bokashi, which provides the microbes that help the compost break down inside. The downside to using a bokashi bin is that you still need to bury the contents outdoors for a couple of weeks after you finish a batch, in order to complete the process. So, it's not an entirely indoor process.

Another type of indoor composter is an electric one that plugs into the wall and sort of mixes and cooks your materials into finished compost.

# CHAPTER 17: COMPANION PLANTING

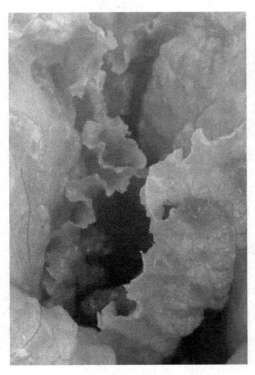 

The idea of companion planting has been providing excellent results to the container farmers. It involves the planting combinations of specific plants for the mutual benefits of the plants involved. The concept here is that individual plants do help each other in taking up nutrients and helping with the management of pests, while also attracting pollinators. Nevertheless, researches are still on the way to find out more planting combination that works fine. There are a few that are listed here that have been scientifically proven and will also work fine in your container garden.

## Melons or squash with Flowering Herbs

All the vegetables here are known to need pollinators for production. Therefore, you can plant flowering herbs such as fennel, parsley, and dill close to the squash or melon to invite insect visitors into your garden. The only way to get enough yields of these vegetables is through pollination.

## Calendula with Broccoli

Calendula flowers are known to produce a sticky substance from their stems which in turn attracts aphids and gets them trapped there. Planting them next to brassica crops such as the broccoli will help to deter aphids from broccoli while also attracting beneficial ladybugs to dine on the aphids.

## Radishes with Carrots

Both radishes and carrots take up nutrients from different locations in the soil, so they do not compete for nutrients or other resources. Their fast growth characterizes radishes, and they do not grow as deeply as carrots do. Carrots generally have long taproots, and it takes more time for them to mature when compared to Radishes.

## Lettuce with Tomatoes or Eggplants

These plants are characterized by different growth habits which makes them beneficial to each other. Tomatoes and eggplants will generally grow taller; thereby, they are useful in shading cool-season crops like lettuce that doesn't like heat at all. Growing them with tomatoes or eggplants will also help in extending their harvest period.

## Nasturtium with Cucumber

This combination involves introducing both pollinators and beneficial insects into your garden, which will, in turn, help in improving biodiversity. Also, Nasturtiums are characterized by a unique scent that helps in repelling pests.

## Tomatoes with Basil or Cilantro

Apart from the belief that planting basil alongside tomatoes helps to improve the flavor of tomatoes, basil also has a strong scent that helps to prevent pests. As an added advantage, when basil or cilantro is allowed to spout flower, it will result in bringing in the pollinators.

## Corn, Pole beans with Squash or Pumpkin

These combinations are popularly referred to as the three sisters. Corn gives pole beans a platform for climbing while beans will convert atmospheric oxygen into a form that can be used by both plants. Squash and pumpkin are leaves spreading plants, thereby creating living mulch that helps in reducing weeds as well as holding of moisture.

## Lettuce with Chives or Garlic

Planting of chives or garlic, which is characterized by strong smell will help in repelling aphids, thus protecting your Lettuce. *You can* also add alyssum nearby to help invite beneficial insects.

## Sweet Alyssum with Swiss chard

Alyssum is an annual crop that can be quickly grown from seed between the rows of vegetables, and it is known to attract hoverflies. The Hoverflies are beneficial insects that help in the control of aphids.

## Chamomile with Cabbage

Chamomile helps in inviting beneficial insects for a variety of brassicas such as cabbage. You can cut off the Chamomile and leave to get decomposed on the bed while allowing the roots to remain intact to decay and help add nutrients to the soil.

## Roses with Geraniums or Chives

Generally, plants that exhibit strong smell or taste will help in deterring aphids and beetle. Though it has not been entirely proven that this works, it worth trying to prevent roses from being eaten by beetle or aphids that multiply rapidly.

# CHAPTER 18: ESSENTIAL TOOLS

OK, now that you have learned about what you can grow and how you can grow them, you'll need the right tools to cultivate your garden. The right tools make gardening much easier and more importantly, more fun! So, these are the tools that every serious gardener should have. There are many tools that you can use for your container gardening but these tools are just enough for your garden and these are:

## Number 1: A watering can

Photo by Muffet on Foter.com / CC BY

As we know plants can't live without water, so instead of using the wine jug from the kitchen, a watering can is much more suitable! Watering cans are useful as you can easily decide how fast you want the water to pour by tipping the can as needed. The long spout is also useful when trying to reach containers that are maybe placed at the back of your garden in a tight space. A nice gentle stream from a watering can is much more appropriate than a gushing mini waterfall from a wine jug. It can really make a mess, believe me, I've tried it! So, invest in a watering can if you don't already own one. You might also want one that has some sort of design on the side as the watering can then become a nice ornament for your garden! A watering can be really helpful for your garden because as a beginner, this will help you give your plants just the right water.

If you are growing in very small containers then a watering can with a pointed snout would probably suit your needs better rather than the one pictured above. You can pick them up on Amazon from anywhere between 5-30 dollars or seek out your local gardening center.

## Number 2: Gloves

This isn't really a must, but I would never garden without mine. They keep your hands and nails from getting dirty, you won't prick your fingers and you can easily pick up a caterpillar and gently place it somewhere else if it is invading your space. Also, some people can be sensitive to some herbs when touching them with their bare hands so it is best to have gloves.

## Number 3: Pruners

Pruners are sharp and allow for a clean-cut, keeping your container plant healthier. If you try cutting them with a knife or scissors you can risk the plant getting infected by the cut not being clean.

Plants have an amazing ability to deal with their wounds. But if you have cut with something other than a pruner, the jagged edges will leave more damaged cells. A sharp pruner is a must!

## Number 4: Garden Trowel

A garden trowel is needed to loosen up the dirt in your containers. Again, you could probably use your fingers for this, but it's not very enjoyable and your fingers and nails will get dirty. I like having a trowel with a red handle instead of something like green, as the red contrasts the plants nicely.

# CONCLUSION

Thank you for making it to the end. Small space or the lack of it should not hinder you from having a garden of your own. If you are living in an apartment or in an area where it seems impossible to have your own garden, then you might decide to forget having one. You might not be interested in starting a garden now; but what if I tell you that you too can grow tasty and succulent produce in a container garden?

Some people think that fruits, vegetables and herbs can only grow in a traditional garden and not in a container garden. The truth is you can grow almost anything in a container garden – the same vegetable, fruit and herb that you can grow in the traditional one. They both follow the same planting methods, caring and maintenance.

It is not a wise idea to grow huge trees in containers because they won't be able to develop properly. You can only grow a huge tree in a container if you turn it into a bonsai, and it will take an ample amount of time and effort before you can have your own bonsai tree. You can choose to plant a dwarf tree which has a DNA that prevents it from growing tall. Choose a dwarf tree if you want to have a tree in a container. The trees that usually have a dwarf version are peaches, apricots, nectarines, apples (but not all varieties of apple) and almonds. The dwarf trees will still bear normal sized fruits.

The benefits that you will reap from container gardening are immeasurable. Why? There are plants that can improve the air circulation in your home, eliminate toxins or give a soothing aromatic scent in your room. You can take your container garden indoors to take advantage of the mentioned benefits and a whole lot more.

They can serve as part of your interior décor, provide fresh herbs ready for picking any time and make your living room practically come alive. You can also choose to have a container garden outside your house. You will never get such benefits if all you have is a traditional garden.

There are also ornamental plants that can give added appeal to your home. If you are having trouble with your interior décor, then it is best to choose gorgeous looking plants to exude the right feeling in the areas that you need to decorate. Plants can blend well with any surrounding or background, but you still need to choose the best plants that will be able to meet the look that you want to achieve.

Remember that there are four different types of container gardens that you can choose from – all can provide the benefits that you don't usually get from a traditional garden. The four types of container garden to choose from are: indoor container garden using soil, fairy garden, indoor garden using the hydroponic system and modified square foot garden.

You can use different containers for your indoor container garden using soil. You can buy your containers in stores, make one or recycle old containers or jars. You can grow fruits, vegetables, ornamental plants and/or herbs. The design for this type of container garden is limited to your imagination. You can choose to have the traditional pots and saucer, hanging, wall-mounted, with a movable frame, or anything that you can think of. You only need to make sure that your plants will be able to get the right amount of light and attention to grow well. You can also put this type of container garden outside your home.

An indoor container garden using a hydroponic system does not use potting soil. This type of indoor container garden uses perlite instead of the usual soil used by the other container gardens.

I hope you have enjoyed this book and that you have learned something.

CPSIA information can be obtained
at www.ICGtesting.com
Printed in the USA
BVHW051035250621
610374BV00009B/1394